Rockets

SPORTS SCIENCE

Science at Work in
BASKETBALL

By Richard Hantula

**Science and Curriculum
Consultant:**
Debra Voege, M.A.,
Science Curriculum
Resource Teacher

Marshall Cavendish
Benchmark
New York

Published by Marshall Cavendish Benchmark
An imprint of Marshall Cavendish Corporation

Other Marshall Cavendish Offices:
Marshall Cavendish International (Asia) Private Limited, 1 New Industrial Road, Singapore 536196 •
Marshall Cavendish International (Thailand) Co Ltd. 253 Asoke, 12th Flr, Sukhumvit 21 Road,
Klongtoey Nua, Wattana, Bangkok 10110, Thailand • Marshall Cavendish (Malaysia) Sdn Bhd,
Times Subang, Lot 46, Subang Hi-Tech Industrial Park, Batu Tiga, 40000 Shah Alam, Selangor
Darul Ehsan, Malaysia

Marshall Cavendish is a trademark of Times Publishing Limited

All websites were available and accurate when this book was sent to press.

Library of Congress Cataloging-in-Publication Data
Hantula, Richard.
        Science at work in basketball / Richard Hantula.
           p. cm. — (Sports science)
        Includes index.
        Summary: "Explains how the laws of science, especially physics, are at
work in the game of basketball"—Provided by publisher.
        ISBN 978-1-60870-588-7 (print) — ISBN 978-1-60870-733-1 (ebook)
        1. Basketball—Juvenile literature. 2. Physics—Juvenile literature. I. Title.
        GV885.1.H337 2012
        796.323—dc22   2010052780

Developed for Marshall Cavendish Benchmark by RJF Publishing LLC (www.RJFpublishing.com)
Design: Westgraphix LLC/Tammy West
Photo Research: Edward A. Thomas

Cover: LeBron James goes up in the air to grab a rebound.

The photographs in this book are used by permission and through the courtesy of:
Front Cover: Mike Ehrmann/Getty Images.
AP Images: Sue Ogrocki, 4; Alex Gallardo, 6; Elaine Thompson, 7; Jim Bryant, 20; NCAA Photos, 24;
Charles Rex Arbogast, 29. Getty Images: Carl Skalak/Sports Illustrated, 10; Andrew D. Bernstein/NBAE, 14;
Heinz Kluetmeier/Sports Illustrated, 18; Newscom: John S Peterson/Icon SMI AYA.

Printed in Malaysia (T)
135642

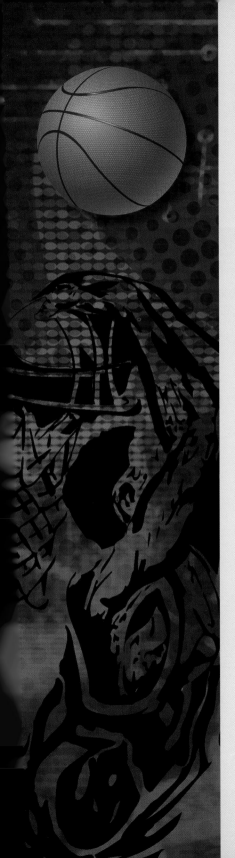

CONTENTS

Chapter One
Air Ball 4

Chapter Two
Gravity Works 10

Chapter Three
Set, Jump, Score 18

Chapter Four
Floor and Rim 24

Glossary 30
Find Out More 31
Index 32

Words defined in the glossary are in **bold** type the first time they appear in the text.

CHAPTER ONE
Air Ball

Kevin Durant leaps high in the air for a dunk shot.

Kobe Bryant of the Los Angeles Lakers is one of the greatest basketball players of all time. In his rookie season (1996–1997) in the National Basketball Association (NBA), he was already a star. His rookie year ended, however, with one of his most famous failures. It came in Game 5 of a playoff series against the Utah Jazz. A loss would eliminate the Lakers from the postseason. With the game winding down, and the win still up for grabs, Bryant attempted three shots. Each time, he completely missed the basket. The Lakers lost.

These **air balls** may have cost the Lakers the game. But they helped create Bryant's reputation for fearless play. Shaquille O'Neal, then the center for the Lakers, later called Bryant "the only guy who had the guts at the time to take shots like that." Of course, the air balls also were a valuable lesson to Bryant. It was a lesson about how important it is to pick your shots carefully.

Air Power

Air balls definitely are not good. Shooters want to make a basket. They want the ball to go to the right place. The same is true of passing. A passer doesn't want to throw the ball past his or her teammate. Practice—and lots of it—is the best way to learn how to shoot well, pass well, and do all the other things that make you a good basketball player. But it also helps to know some basic facts about the ball, about how the ball moves, and also about how a player's body moves.

Some of these facts have to do with what the ball is made of. A basketball is full of air. This air affects how the ball behaves. It helps make the ball springy, or able to bounce well. It also makes the ball light enough to handle

KOBE BRYANT

Kobe Bryant was born in 1978 in Philadelphia, Pennsylvania. His father, Joe Bryant, played in the NBA for several seasons. Later, he played seven seasons in Italy. Kobe's family moved back to the United States when he was 14. In high school, Kobe played all five basketball positions. In his senior year, he led his school to the Pennsylvania state title. He won several national honors.

Bryant took the then-unusual step of skipping college and going straight into professional ball, joining the Lakers in 1997. He went on to help the Lakers win five (as of 2010) NBA titles. He was named the league's Most Valuable Player (MVP) in 2008. He also earned MVP honors in the 2009 and 2010 postseason finals.

easily. A solid rubber ball the size of a basketball might bounce well, but it would be too heavy to play with.

The air outside the ball is important, too. When a player shoots or passes the ball, it moves through the air. The air affects the ball's movement. For example, it pushes against the ball. This causes the ball to go a little slower than if there were no air. This **resistance** by the air to the ball's movement is called **drag**. In many basketball situations, drag is not very strong. It is often stronger in sports such as baseball where the ball can move extremely fast. Still, drag has some effect on a moving basketball.

Forces at Work

Air resistance is an example of a **force**. A force is simply a push or a pull. Forces make the game of basketball—and everything else—possible. Earth's **gravity**, which pulls objects downward, is a force that is always there. It acts on objects all the time. Other forces that are important in basketball act for only a short time. When players shoot or pass the ball, they change its movement by applying a force.

A special branch of science studies forces and the movement of objects. It is called **physics**. Physicists—scientists who specialize in physics—have discovered that all objects in the world obey certain rules, or laws, when

As soon as a player throws the ball, gravity starts pulling it down. Shown here: Lauren Jackson gets a pass off past a defender.

ISAAC NEWTON

Isaac Newton was born in 1643 in Lincolnshire, England. His father, a farmer, died a few months before Isaac was born. His family tried to get the teenaged Isaac to take up farming, but he was not very good at it. He went to Cambridge University, where he got interested in mathematics and science.

Newton eventually became a professor at Cambridge. Later, he moved to London, where he became president of the Royal Society, England's main scientific society. He made many discoveries in math and science. In physics, he came up with the three laws of motion and described the workings of Earth's gravity. According to legend, he began thinking about gravity when he saw an apple fall. Newton died in 1727.

forces act on them. Three key laws were described by the English scientist Isaac Newton in the 1600s.

PHYSICS FACT

First Law of Motion

If an object is at rest, it will stay at rest unless a force acts on it. If an object is moving, it will keep on moving in the same direction and at the same speed unless a force acts on it.

First Law of Motion

The first of Newton's three laws says that an object's speed or its direction of movement can change only if a force acts on it. Take, for example, a moving ball. It will keep on going at the same speed and in the same direction forever unless some force causes a change. The same idea applies to a ball or other object that is not moving. Such an object has zero speed and is said to be at rest. An object at rest will start moving only if some force causes it to.

Of course, on Earth a real ball that is moving through the air sooner or later always comes to a stop. This is because forces act on it. Earth's gravity pulls it down. Air

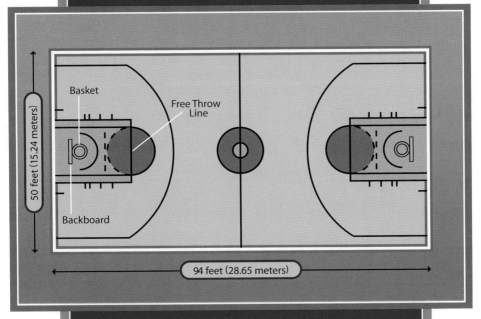

NBA Basketball Court

Basket

Free Throw Line

50 feet (15.24 meters)

Backboard

94 feet (28.65 meters)

NBA players apply a force to the ball when they shoot a basket or move the ball down the 94-foot court.

resistance slows it down. If one player passes the ball, the player making the catch stops the ball by applying force.

Some people use the word *velocity* to mean simply "speed." For a physicist, however, velocity has a special meaning. It is the combination of speed and direction. Using *velocity* in this way makes it possible to say the first law of motion very simply: an object will change its velocity only if a force acts on it.

There's another way the first law is sometimes explained. This uses the idea of **inertia**. Inertia is resistance to a change in movement. It is because of inertia that changing an object's state of motion requires the use of a force.

CHAPTER TWO

Gravity Works

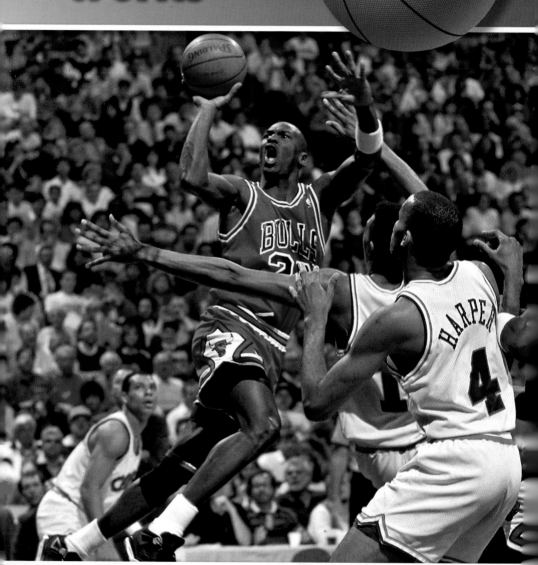

Michael Jordan soars above the opposition for a shot during Game 5 of the 1989 playoff series against the Cleveland Cavaliers.

It went down in history as "The Shot." In 1989, Michael Jordan and his Chicago Bulls had not yet won any NBA titles. They did make it into the playoffs that year. Their first-round opponent was the Cleveland Cavaliers, who had finished ahead of the Bulls in the regular-season standings. Chicago and Cleveland fought hard right up to the closing seconds of the fifth and deciding game of the series. Jordan got the ball, dribbled for position, and jumped in order to take a shot. Craig Ehlo, one of Cleveland's best defenders, also jumped, trying for the block. Jordan waited, seeming to hang in the air, until Ehlo was no longer in the way, and then he shot. The ball went through the net, and the Bulls won. The victory was a sign they were moving up in the basketball world. Just two years later, Jordan led them to their first NBA title.

MICHAEL JORDAN

The NBA website calls Michael Jordan the greatest basketball player ever. A star on both offense and defense, he gained the nicknames "His Airness" and "Air Jordan" because he seemed to have the ability to remain in the air an unusually long time when he jumped.

Jordan was born in 1963 in Brooklyn, New York. His family soon moved to Wilmington, North Carolina. There, he played on his high school's junior varsity and then varsity basketball team. He played college ball at the University of North Carolina, helping the team win the national title in 1982.

When Jordan turned pro, he joined the NBA's Chicago Bulls. He led the Bulls to three straight NBA titles in 1991, 1992, and 1993. Then he retired. After trying his hand at baseball, he returned to the Bulls and led them to another three straight titles in 1996, 1997, and 1998. In all six championship finals, he was named the MVP. Five times during his career he was named the league's MVP (1988, 1991, 1992, 1996, and 1998).

Can't Beat Physics

Michael Jordan was a very talented player, but he didn't actually stay in the air longer than any other good jumper. Even he couldn't break the laws of physics. Earth's gravity pulls on him as it does on everyone and everything else. When basketball players jump, they usually get no more than about 3 feet (90 centimeters) above the floor before they start going down. If they jump really hard, they may go as high as 4 feet (120 centimeters), but that's unusual. The hang time for a 4-foot jump is about one second, no matter who jumps. The hang time for a 3-foot jump is a little less.

Jumpers like Jordan only look like they have a long hang time. In other words, their long hang time is an **illusion**. One thing that makes their hang time seem longer is that they hold on to the ball longer. They often don't shoot the ball until they are going back down. Jordan often pulled his legs up during a jump. This also made it seem he was staying really high. Stretching out an arm or moving the ball around during the jump can make the hang time seem longer, too.

Up and Down

Players don't always jump straight up when they shoot. Sometimes they move forward or backward as well as up. But that doesn't make any difference as to how long they stay in the air. This is because gravity pulls straight down. When players don't jump straight up, their motion actually has two parts. One is an upward, or vertical, velocity. The other is a velocity in a horizontal direction—that is, parallel with the floor. Gravity doesn't work horizontally. It pulls only downward. So it affects only the vertical part of a player's jump. Since gravity controls how long a player stays above the floor, the player's horizontal motion, if any, does not affect the hang time.

Jump Force

In order to jump, a player has to apply a force to the floor. It doesn't matter whether the player is running or standing still. The jump is a change in the player's motion. This, says Newton's first law, requires use of a force. Of course, how high a jumper goes will depend on how strong the force is. The harder that jumpers push against the floor, the higher they can go before gravity pulls them back down.

But the height of a jump doesn't depend only on the amount of force. It also depends on the jumper's **mass**. Mass is simply the amount of matter an object has. Heavy objects have more mass than light ones. If two players, one heavy and one not so heavy, use the same force in jumping, the lighter one will go higher. Newton came up with a second law that describes this and similar situations.

Second Law of Motion

Newton's second law deals with how a force changes an object's motion. It makes use of the idea of **acceleration**. In everyday life, people often use the word *acceleration* to mean "speeding up." But in physics, acceleration means

PHYSICS FACT

Second Law of Motion
When a force acts on an object, the greater the force, the greater the acceleration it gives to the object. Also, if the same force is used on objects of different mass, objects with less mass receive more acceleration.

any change in the velocity of an object. The change may be an increase or a decrease in speed, a change in direction, or a change in both speed and direction.

The second law of motion says that the acceleration an object receives from a force depends on two things. One is the size of the force. For any object, a stronger force will give it more acceleration. In other words, the more force Kobe Bryant uses when he makes a jump, the faster his velocity will be when he leaves the ground. The faster the velocity, the higher he will go before starting to come back down.

The second thing that affects acceleration is the mass of the object. For any force, an object with less mass will receive more acceleration than an object with more mass. If Tracy McGrady and Yao Ming each did a jump using the same amount of force, McGrady would go higher. That's because Yao Ming is the bigger, more massive player. It is hard for really big players like Yao to jump high. They need to use a lot of force to move their mass.

Yao Ming (right) has more mass than Tracy McGrady (left). For the two players to jump to the same height, Yao would have to use a lot more force.

Light and Heavy

People sometimes use an object's weight to describe how much mass it has. Weight and mass are related, but they actually are different things. Mass is the amount of matter the object has. Weight is a measure of gravity's pull on the object. Gravity's pull depends on the object's mass. So it makes sense to say that an object weighing 6 pounds (2.70 kilograms) has more mass than an object weighing 3 pounds (1.35 kilograms).

But this gravity is the gravitational pull of Earth. Other bodies in the universe have a different gravity. For example, the Moon's gravitational pull is weaker than Earth's. If an object that weighs 6 pounds on Earth is taken to the Moon, it will weigh only about 1 pound (0.45 kilogram) there, even though its mass will be the same. Because of the difference in gravity, a basketball on the Moon won't fall to the ground as fast as it does on Earth.

Weight on Earth and the Moon

Moon

Earth

6

1

A book that weighs 6 pounds on Earth will weigh only 1 pound on the Moon because of the Moon's weaker gravity.

Force Against Force

When more than one force acts on an object, the object's motion will be a combination of the effects from each force. Sometimes forces cancel each other out. This is what happens when a basketball lies on the ground. Gravity keeps pulling it downward, but the ball doesn't move, because the ground pushes back with an equal force. The two forces are exactly balanced.

Jumping is a different story. When players jump, they push into the floor with enough force to overcome gravity. They leave the floor with a certain **momentum**. Momentum is a way of measuring motion. It depends on both velocity and mass.

But as soon as players leave the floor, their velocity starts decreasing. The main cause for the drop in velocity is gravity. Gravity never stops pulling downward. It causes jumpers to gradually lose momentum as they rise. At some point their momentum is no longer enough to overcome gravity, and they start going back down. As they drop, they go faster and faster, because gravity keeps accelerating them.

Third Law of Motion

Newton described another law of motion that helps explain the forces at work when a person jumps. This third law of motion says every action has an equal and opposite reaction. In other words, when one object applies a force to

PHYSICS FACT

Third Law of Motion

When one object applies a force to a second object, the second also applies an equal force to the first. In other words, for every action there is an equal and opposite reaction.

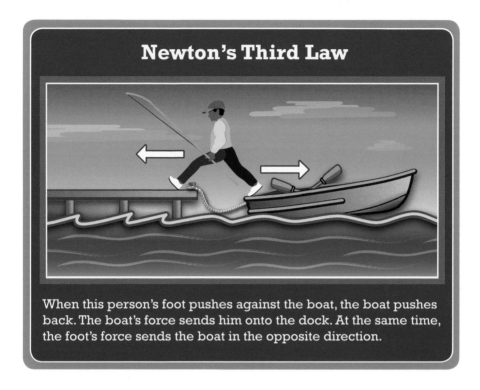

Newton's Third Law

When this person's foot pushes against the boat, the boat pushes back. The boat's force sends him onto the dock. At the same time, the foot's force sends the boat in the opposite direction.

another, the second object also applies a force to the first. The two forces are equal in amount, but they act in opposite directions.

A jumper pushes into the ground with a certain force. The ground pushes back with an equal force. The ground is part of Earth, which is far too big to be moved by the force exerted by the jumper. (Remember, Newton's second law says that the greater the mass of an object, the smaller the acceleration it will get from a given force.) The jumper rises because of the reaction force from the ground.

The situation is a little different for a jump from a movable object such as a small boat. When a person jumps out of a small boat, the boat moves away. This is the third law of motion at work. Unlike Earth, the boat is not too big to be pushed away by the jumper's force.

CHAPTER THREE

Set, Jump, Score

Michael Jordan goes up for the winning basket in the 1982 college basketball men's national championship game.

Michael Jordan was a great shooter. His NBA scoring average—more than 30 points per game—remains the highest in league history. He started making his reputation as a reliable crunch-time player long before he turned pro. In early 1982, while still a freshman at North Carolina, he made the winning shot in the national championship game with just 15 seconds left on the clock. Georgetown was ahead, 62–61, and North Carolina had the ball. Jordan moved to the left side of the court, received a pass, squared up, and coolly made a perfect 16-foot (4.9-meter) jump shot.

Far and Near

The jump shot is one of the most popular shots today. The shooter jumps and sends the ball toward the basket. After the shooter releases the ball, it travels in a curved path, or an arc. It moves first upward and then downward, ending up (the shooter hopes) in the basket. A jump shot can be hard for a defender to stop, since a shooter with good jumping ability and timing may be able to shoot right over a defender. Also, a jump shot can be done while a player is on the move.

Advantages like these explain why the jump shot has largely replaced, at least in the pros, the once-popular set shot. A set shot is like a jump shot except that it is made while the shooter is standing still with his or her feet on the ground. Because the set shot is easier to defend against, its main use today is in shooting free throws.

In a set shot or a jump shot, the ball acts like any object that is thrown or shot into the air. Scientists call such an object a **projectile**. The object begins with a certain momentum that it got from the force that threw or shot it. After that, the main forces governing the ball's motion are gravity and forces

Diana Taurasi is about to launch a shot in a Women's National Basketball Association game.

connected with the air, such as drag.

Other popular basketball shots are done close to the basket. They do not use the ball as a projectile. The slam dunk, for instance, involves jumping up and simply slamming the ball down through the hoop. In a layup, a player lays the ball up and into the hoop, either directly or by banking, or bouncing, the ball off the backboard.

Cannonballs, Fly Balls, and Basketballs

It is easy to find examples of projectiles. A fly ball in baseball is a projectile. A cannonball fired from a cannon is a projectile. A basketball passed from one player to another is also a projectile. When a projectile begins its flight, it has a certain velocity—that is, it is headed in a certain direction at a certain speed. To understand what happens to the projectile, it helps to look at each of the two separate parts that make up its overall velocity. One of these parts is velocity in a horizontal direction. The other is velocity in a vertical direction.

Gravity keeps pulling on the projectile. Its pull is always downward. It acts on the projectile's vertical velocity only. It

Velocity of a Jump Shot

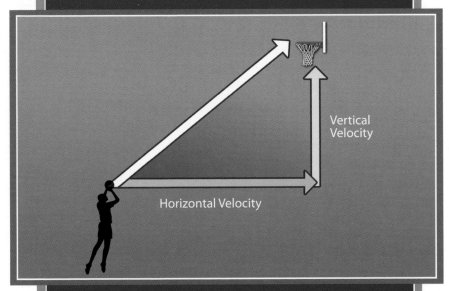

Vertical Velocity

Horizontal Velocity

The velocity of a jump shot thrown toward the basket has two parts. One is the ball's vertical, or upward, velocity. The other is the ball's horizontal, or forward, velocity.

has no effect on horizontal velocity. Gravity begins changing the vertical velocity as soon as the projectile starts its flight.

Aiming Up

If the projectile is shot flat—parallel to the ground—its starting velocity is all horizontal. It has no vertical velocity, at least at first. Gravity's pull immediately makes it start dropping toward the ground. The projectile won't travel very far. It will quickly land on the ground—unless it hits something or is caught.

For this reason, projectiles that need to go a long way— such as cannonballs and long passes in basketball—are aimed somewhat upward. Jump shots are also aimed upward, because they need to make it to the height of the basket.

Playing the Angles

When taking a set shot or a jump shot, is it better to shoot the ball really high or more flat? What launch angle—the angle between the floor and the ball's path as it leaves the shooter's hands—is best?

One way to try to figure out the answer is to imagine what the basket's rim looks like to the ball as it approaches. The rim is a circle roughly twice the size of the ball. When the ball comes straight down, as in a slam dunk, it "sees" the rim as a big circle below it. The circle is easy to hit. Slam dunks rarely miss.

With a jump shot, however, the ball has to be shot in an extremely high arc for it to come almost straight down on the basket. With such a high arc, the ball will come down very fast, making it likely to bounce far away if it happens to be slightly off target. A slower shot is generally preferable, since it has better odds of making it into the hoop if it happens to hit the rim or backboard. So an extremely high arc is not usually a good idea for a jump shot.

On the other hand, if the ball comes in along a very flat arc, it sees the hoop as a squashed oval, impossible to fit into. It's best if the ball comes in at an angle between these two extremes—around 45 degrees. Usually, shooters can achieve this with a launch angle of a little bit more than 45 degrees.

Projectiles like these start out with a vertical velocity as well as a horizontal one. Because gravity has to overcome the upward velocity, the projectile travels farther before landing.

In the first part of its flight, gravity makes the upward velocity get smaller and smaller. At some point this velocity becomes zero. Because gravity keeps pulling, the projectile starts falling toward the ground. Gravity now works to increase its downward velocity. As a result, the path traveled by the projectile is an arc that goes first upward, then downward.

Drag and Turn

The air's effects on a basketball's flight are sometimes very noticeable. Drag tries to make the ball slow down. Newton's third law of motion explains why this happens. As the ball moves forward, it pushes particles of air out of its way. In other words, it exerts a force on the air. The air obeys the third law of motion and pushes back on the ball. The faster the ball goes, the greater the force it exerts on the air. But if the ball's force is greater, the reaction force from the air will be greater, too. That is why drag becomes stronger at high speeds.

Another type of force connected with the air results from a basketball's spin. Usually a basketball flying through the air has some spin. The ball rotates around an imaginary line called the **axis** that runs through its center. This spin may act together with the air to produce a force called the **Magnus force**.

This force results from changes that spin causes in air pressure close to the ball. Normally the air at Earth's surface pushes on everything with a force of about 14.7 pounds per square inch (1 kilogram per square centimeter). People don't usually notice this force, called air pressure, because they are used to it.

When a spinning ball flies through the air, the spin changes the air pressure right next to the ball. Because of the spin, the air flowing by moves faster on one side of the ball and slower on the other. The pressure is higher on the side with slower air flow. This pressure difference bends the ball's path.

Suppose the ball has **backspin**. In this type of spin, the back of the ball rolls down and to the front. The air flows faster on the top of the ball and slower on the bottom. This makes the air pressure higher on the bottom of the ball. The result is a small force pushing upward. Because of this lift force, the ball falls more slowly than it otherwise would. When a player makes a long pass down the court, the ball usually gets backspin. A fast backspin may help keep the ball in the air a little longer.

CHAPTER FOUR

Floor and Rim

The forces of gravity and friction are at work when a player runs and dribbles. Shown here: Jeanette Pohlen, playing for Stanford University, moves the ball downcourt in a 2010 game.

The guard gets the ball. She sees an opening and starts to drive through the other team's defenders. Twisting and turning, she dribbles her way toward the basket. She stops. She shoots. The ball hits the rim, bounces up, and then drops into the hoop for a score.

A lot of things had to happen in order to get those two points. They all depend on forces that follow the laws of physics. Some of these laws were at work when the ball bounced off the floor or the basket rim. The guard's quick footwork to avoid the defenders was possible because gravity's downward pull kept her from floating off into space. Gravity was not the only force that helped her to keep her footing. **Friction** between her shoes and the floor helped, too. Friction is a resistance that an object experiences when it tries to move across a surface. It was friction between the guard's hands and the ball that let her keep the ball under control. Friction kept the ball from slipping away from her.

Bouncing Ball

When a ball falls to the floor, it bounces. The third law of motion explains why. When the ball hits the floor, it pushes down on the floor with a force. The floor reacts by pushing upward with a force of equal strength. The floor makes the ball move. It causes the ball to go up.

If a ball bounces by itself more than once, it goes less high after each bounce. The reason for this is that something happens to the ball's **energy**. Energy is the ability to do work. It exists in different forms. For instance, a moving object has a form of energy called **kinetic energy**. When the ball bounces, it loses some kinetic energy.

PHYSICS FACT

Energy

Energy comes in different forms. Heat is a form of energy. So is light. Kinetic energy is another example of a form of energy. There's an important rule of physics called the law of **conservation** of energy:

Energy cannot be destroyed. It can, however, be changed from one form to another.

One of the basic laws of physics says that energy cannot be created or destroyed. It can, however, be changed into a different form. That is what happens when the ball bounces. As it hits the floor, it gets squished out of shape. It quickly regains its normal shape and bobs back up. In the process, some of the ball's original energy gets changed into other forms, such as heat energy. As a result, the rising ball has less kinetic energy. It won't go as high as before. In addition, the ball loses a little kinetic energy in opposing the air's resistance to it. If the bouncing continues, the ball will eventually lose all of its kinetic energy and come to a stop.

Dribbling is a different story. When basketball players dribble, they apply a force to the ball at the top of each bounce. This force accelerates the ball, giving it additional kinetic energy. So dribbling can go on forever—or at least until the player gets tired!

Spin and Bounce

A ball's spin affects the way it moves after it bounces. Basketball players often make good use of this fact when throwing a bounce pass or shooting the ball.

Whenever a ball hits a surface, such as the floor or the backboard, friction resists the ball's motion. So friction also changes in some way how the ball moves.

Suppose a basketball player throws a bounce pass without using any spin at all. When the ball hits the floor, it will bounce away at an angle about the same as the one at which it hit the floor. At the same time, friction causes the ball to lose a little speed going forward, and it gives the ball **topspin**. (In topspin, the top of the ball spins forward and down. Topspin is the opposite of backspin.) The topspin happens because only the bottom of the ball touches the floor and meets resistance. Friction doesn't affect the rest of the ball, which continues to move. As a result, the ball begins to roll, producing a topspin.

By snapping his or her wrists backward or forward when finishing the throw, a player can throw a bounce pass with either backspin or topspin. If the ball has backspin when it hits the floor, it meets more friction than does a ball with no spin. The friction from the floor resists both the ball's spin and the ball's forward motion. It noticeably reduces both the ball's rate of spin and the ball's forward speed. It may even change the backspin to topspin. It also causes the angle at which the ball bounces from the floor to be larger than

Spin Affects How the Ball Bounces

No spin   Backspin   Topsin

The way a bounce pass is thrown—with no spin, topspin, or backspin—affects how the ball comes up to the receiver.

Topspin can make a bounce pass travel farther. Backspin can make it easier to catch.

the angle at which it hit the floor.

When a ball with topspin hits the floor, it will bounce away at an angle smaller than the one at which it hit. With very fast topspin, the ball may even gain speed from the bounce.

A basketball player who wants to throw a long bounce pass may decide to give the ball topspin, because that will help it travel more distance. In other situations, putting backspin on the throw may be better. The ball bounces up to the receiver, and its spin after the bounce is slow. These things make the ball easier to catch.

Spin and Basket

Spin can also play a role in shooting the ball. Backspin, for instance, is useful in jump shots and free throws. To see why, it helps to look at the horizontal and vertical parts of the ball's velocity. If the ball bounces against the backboard or basket rim, the backspin will lessen the horizontal velocity. This makes the vertical velocity play a greater role in the ball's overall velocity. As a result, the bounce becomes more vertical. This is a good thing. It makes the ball more likely to fall into the basket.

Topspin comes in handy when a player goes under the basket and tries to make a "reverse" layup. Giving the ball topspin can help it bounce off the backboard into the basket.

Sticky Force

Friction acts like a sticky force. It resists the motion of an object across a surface. Without friction, it would be impossible to walk. People walk by pushing backward with each foot against the ground. Without friction, a person's foot would just slip backward. The person's body would not move forward.

Actually, there are two kinds of friction, called static and kinetic. When an object tries to move across a surface, the static friction from the surface holds the object in place without slipping—at least it does this as long as the force applied by the object doesn't get too strong. If the force reaches a certain level, the object will start to slip.

The surface still offers some resistance to the slipping object. This resistance, called kinetic friction, is usually weaker than static friction.

It is thanks to friction that basketball players can run, cut, turn, drive, and stop so quickly on the court.

Luol Deng shoots a reverse layup from under the basket.

GLOSSARY

acceleration: A change in velocity. As a measurement, it is the rate at which velocity changes.

air ball: A shot that not only misses the basket but also doesn't even hit the rim or the backboard.

axis: In a spinning ball, the line running through the ball's center around which the ball turns.

backspin: A type of spin in which the back of a ball rolls down and toward the front. It is the opposite of topspin.

conservation: In physics, the idea that something cannot be destroyed. For example, energy is always conserved, but it may change from one form to another.

drag: Air resistance; a force that slows an object moving through the air.

energy: In physics, the ability to do work.

force: Anything that causes a change in the velocity of an object, such as a push or a pull.

friction: A force resisting the movement of an object across a surface.

gravity: A force that pulls objects toward the center of Earth.

illusion: Something that isn't actually the way it seems or appears.

inertia: The tendency of an object to resist being accelerated. A force has to be applied in order to put into motion an object that is at rest or to change the velocity of an object that is moving.

kinetic energy: The energy of a moving object.

Magnus force: A force that acts on a moving object that is rapidly spinning. It pushes the object sideways relative to the axis of the spin.

mass: The amount of matter in an object.

momentum: A measure of an object's motion. It equals the object's mass multiplied by its velocity.

physics: The branch of science dealing with matter and energy. Scientists who work in physics are called physicists. They study such things as moving objects.

projectile: An object that has been put into motion in the air by some force.

resistance: Opposition to the movement of an object.

topspin: A type of spin in which the front of a ball rolls down and toward the back. It is the opposite of backspin.

velocity: In physics, the speed and direction of a moving object. Some people use the word to mean simply "speed."

FIND OUT MORE

BOOKS

Gardner, Robert, and Dennis Shortelle. *Slam Dunk! Science Projects with Basketball.* Berkeley Heights, NJ: Enslow, 2009.

Hareas, John. *Basketball.* New York: DK Eyewitness Books, 2005.

Labrecque, Ellen. *Basketball.* Ann Arbor, MI: Cherry Lake, 2009.

Slade, Suzanne. *Basketball: How It Works.* Mankato, MN: Capstone Press, 2010.

WEBSITES

www.fearofphysics.com/Proj/proj.html
This site features a game that shows how shots are affected by distance from the basket, the height of shooter, the speed of ball, and the angle of the shot.

www.nba.com
This is the official site of the National Basketball Association. It is packed with statistics and news relating to the NBA. The section NBA 101 includes coverage of the league's history and rules.

http://pbskids.org/dragonflytv/show/basketball.html
This page from the site for the television program *DragonflyTV* gives ideas for scientifically studying different factors that affect shooting. It includes a video clip of an experiment done by two kids.

www.topendsports.com/sport/basketball
The Topend Sports website, which originated in Australia, has a lot of information about the basics of basketball, including some physics pointers.

INDEX

Page numbers in **bold** type are for photos, charts, and illustrations.

acceleration, 13–14, 17
air balls, 5
air pressure, 23
air resistance (drag), 6, 7, 22–23
axis, 23

backspin, 23, 27, **27**, 28
bounce passes. *See* passes
Bryant, Kobe, 5, 6, **6**, 14

conservation of energy, 26
court (basketball), **9**

defenders (basketball players),
   7, 11, 19, 25
Deng, Luol, **29**
drag. *See* air resistance (drag)
dribbling, **24**, 25–26
dunk shot. *See* slam dunk
Durant, Kevin, **4**

Ehlo, Craig, 11
energy, 25–26

first law of motion, 8–9
force (physics), 7–9, 13–14,
   16–17, **17**, 19–20, 22–23,
   24, 25, 29
friction, **24**, 25, 27, 29

gravity, 7, **7**, 8, 12, 13, 15, 16,
   19–22, **24**, 25

hang time, 12
horizontal motion (velocity), 12–13,
   20–22, **21**, 28

inertia, 9

Jackson, Lauren, **7**
Jordan, Michael, **10**, 11, 12, **18**, 19
jump shots, **18**, 19, 21, **21**, 22

jumps and jumping, **4**, **10**, 11, 12–13,
   14, **14**, 16, 17, 19
kinetic energy, 25–26

launch angle, 22

Magnus force, 23
mass, 13–14, **14**, 15, 16, 17
McGrady, Tracy, 14, **14**
momentum, 16, 19
Moon, 15, **15**

Newton, Isaac, 8, 13, 16–17, **17**,
   22–23

passes, 7, **7**, 21, 23, 26–28, **27**, **28**
Pohlen, Jeanette, **24**
projectiles, 19–22

rest (physics), 8
reverse layup, 29, **29**

second law of motion, 13–14, 17
set shot, 19, 22
shots, types of, **4**, **18**, 19, 20, **20**, 21,
   21, 22, 29, **29**
slam dunk, **4**, 20, 22
spin (on basketball), 23, 26, 27, **27**,
   28, **28**, 29

Taurasi, Diana, **20**
third law of motion, 16–17, **17**,
   22–23, 25
topspin, 27, **27**, 28, 29

velocity, 9, 12–13, 14, 16, 20–22,
   21, 28
vertical motion (velocity), 12–13,
   20–22, **21**, 28

weight, 15, **15**

Yao Ming, 14, **14**

About the Author

Richard Hantula has written, edited, and translated books and articles on science and technology for more than three decades. He was the senior U.S. editor for the *Macmillan Encyclopedia of Science.*